Nowhere is safe in Gaza

Feisal G. Mohamed

Nowhere is safe in Gaza

An erasure poem using as source text
South Africa's Application Instituting Proceedings against Israel
for Violations of the Genocide Convention
International Court of Justice
29 December 2023

BRICK BOOKS
PRINCE EDWARD COUNTY, ONTARIO

Library and Archives Canada Cataloguing in Publication
Title: Nowhere is safe in Gaza : an erasure of South Africa's
   application instituting proceedings against Israel for violations
   of the Genocide Convention, International Court of Justice,
   29 December 2023 / by Feisal G. Mohamed.
Names: Mohamed, Feisal G. (Feisal Gharib), 1974– author
Identifiers: Canadiana (print) 20250324717 | Canadiana
   (ebook) 20250324822 | ISBN 9781771316736 (softcover) |
   ISBN 9781771316743 (EPUB) | ISBN 9781771316750 (PDF)
Subjects: LCSH: Israel-Hamas War, 2023-–Poetry. | LCSH:
   Gaza Strip–History–Bombardment, 2023-–Poetry. | LCSH:
   Genocide–Gaza Strip–Poetry. | LCGFT: Found poetry. |
   LCGFT: Visual poetry.
Classification: LCC PS8626.O44734 N69 2026 | DDC C811/.6–dc23

We gratefully acknowledge the Canada Council for the Arts,
the Government of Canada through the Canada Book Fund,
the Ontario Arts Council, and the Government of Ontario for
their support of our publishing program.

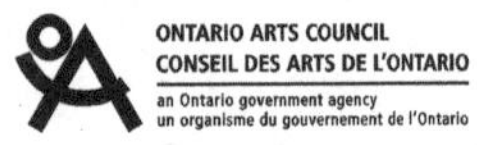  
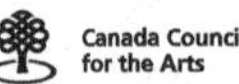 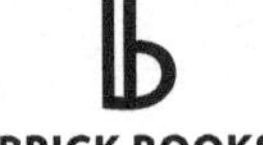

Edited by Jordan Abel.
Author photo by Sally Fattah.
The book is set in Suisse Works.

BRICK BOOKS
www.brickbooks.ca

Though much of the work of Brick Books takes place on
the ancestral lands of the Anishinaabeg, Haudenosaunee,
Huron-Wendat, and Mississaugas of the Credit peoples,
our editors, authors, and readers from many backgrounds
are situated from coast to coast to coast in Canada on the
traditional and unceded territories of over six hundred nations
who have cared for Turtle Island from time immemorial.
While living and working on these lands, we are committed
to hearing and returning the rightful imaginative space to
the poetries, songs, and stories that have been untold, under-
told, wrongly told, and suppressed through colonization.

for the

Palestinians of Gaza

past, present,

and future

PREFACE

"South Africa's action against Israel seems to have opened a new era in the relations between the Global North and the Global South, and the symbolic impact is profound."
—*Francesca Albanese, UN Special Rapporteur on the Palestinian Territories*

"Genocide means… deliberately inflicting on the group conditions of life calculated to bring about its physical destruction in whole or in part."
—*Genocide Convention, Article II(c)*

With its application to the International Court of Justice on December 29, 2023, South Africa launched a quiet revolution. That this occurred in the decorous and ceremony-bound halls of the world's highest court should not blind us to its subversive realignment of global legal order. Within the confines of an international system often, and not unjustly, accused of a neo-colonial ethos lending a patina of legitimacy to the hypocrisies of the "free world," South Africa emerges as a champion of the stateless. A government born of resistance to apartheid takes up the Palestinian cause, using its hard-won status as sovereign nation, and thus as juridical person in international law, to advocate on behalf of a people being ground under the heel of the West's most darling satellite state. In the weeks following the application, the justices of the court approved some of the provisional measures requested, accepting that Israel's actions do indeed fall within the scope of the Genocide Convention, with final determination on the question of violations to follow.

For Israel, of course, the historical arc is quite different: the Jewish state born in the wake of the Holocaust now charged with genocide, with the ghoulish declarations of its politicians, army leadership, and common soldiers assembled and brought to light. The Genocide Convention, which came into being through the indefatigable efforts of Raphael Lemkin—the Polish jurist who coined the term genocide, whose entire family was murdered in the Holocaust, and who makes a brief cameo appearance in the South African filing—becomes the mechanism for exposing Israeli crimes. In the current government's view of history, Israel is incapable of genocide. "The charge of genocide leveled against Israel is not only false," remarked Benyamin Netanyahu, "it's outrageous, and decent people everywhere should reject it." Israel was untroubled by the ICJ's approval of some provisional measures requested by South Africa: rather than reevaluating its actions in Gaza, it took aim at UNRWA—the "primary platform for humanitarian assistance to over 2.2 million people in Gaza," as it is put in these pages—claiming that a dozen or so of its thousands of Palestinian workers took part in the attacks of October 7. And rather than taking pause, and taking seriously their duty to prevent and punish genocide, Israel's enablers in the West immediately withheld funding for UNRWA during Gaza's greatest hour of need.

While the Holocaust always enters our minds when the question of genocide is raised, we err if we think no further in our reckoning with genocide as historical phenomenon and as legal category. One point of having an international convention is to push aside imprecise and politically malleable historical analogy in favor of normative rules reflecting global consensus. Nothing in the South African application demands that we see the genocide of Palestinians in Gaza as parallel to the Holocaust, nor that we see the current regime in Israel as equivalent to the Nazis. Coming to terms with events in Bosnia, Rwanda, and Sudan have all left their mark on the legal and ethical dimensions of genocide. South Africa's action persuasively claims a place for Gaza in this evolving definition, lifting the question out of the casual and hyper-partisan discourse of our moment and into the realm of international law. Despite these many claims to our attention, and despite the ready availability of the text on the ICJ website, this legal filing is not likely to reach a broad audience. It is the fate of documents entering the UN orbit to be widely ignored despite their significance—reports on climate come to mind.

As someone with standing interests in international humanitarian law and the politics of the Middle East, I was glued to every one of the eighty-four pages of the original. Living and working in the United States, an investment in international law can feel like the idle pursuit of a quixotic naif, much more so than in Canada, where I was born and educated. My father emigrated from Egypt in the weeks following the Six-Day War. Israel's expansion in that conflict included not only the Palestinian territories occupied to this day, but also Egyptian land up to the Suez Canal. Port Said, where my parents grew up, became a front line, and my then-teenaged mother was sent with her sisters to live in Cairo, at a safe distance from further conflict. After another war in 1973, the year before I was born, and the signing of a peace treaty that is one of my earliest childhood memories, Egypt regained territory lost in 1967—except for Gaza, on which Sadat settled for assurances of a soon-to-be-formed Palestinian state. Growing up in Canada, the unsettled Palestinian question felt for me both far and near, a remote experience also tied in some way to my personal and family history and to my outlook on the region. Always the lingering questions on the Palestinian cause: *Should I do more? Should Egypt do more? Should the world do more?* Since October 2023, the genocide in Gaza and accelerated ethnic cleansing of the West Bank have answered these with a thundering *YES*.

The literary potential of the South African filing was immediately apparent. Erasure occurred to me as a fitting representation of the

invisible visibility of the document itself and of events in Gaza,
both hypervisible and being actively hidden by those perpetrating,
and jusitfying, slaughter and deprivation. Even as the text makes
clear Israel's efforts to destroy evidence of its current actions—
including killing and disappearing journalists, aid workers, and
medical staff—the story is being told. In the current text erasure is
an archeological device, excavating and amplifying human voices
and experiences from the formal and verbal conventions of a legal
document. Experienced UN bureaucrats who have spent decades-
long careers observing the consequences of war and famine tell us
that the suffering in Gaza is unprecedented, and time and again
issue desperate *cris de coeur.* We hear the voices of Palestinians
on the ground, and are given sketches of doctors and academics,
local heroes and children who have been slaughtered: names and
personalities emerge from statistics and rubble. And we hear the
menacing chorus of *génocidaires* in Israel's government and military,
whose words spill like poison into a civil society all too eager to
repeat them. Erasure dims the language of legal procedure. What
remains is what must not be erased: the experiences of Palestinians
and the record of Palestinian life in Gaza; the heroism of aid workers,
health workers, and journalists; the words of Israeli officials making
their intentions crystal clear.

Every word of the present text arises from the original legal
document, as do instances of italic and boldface type. Page breaks
and spaces between lines of text have been altered to meet the needs
of this erasure, but the place of each word in each line of text has
been preserved. Which is to say that if words from the South African
filing and this text were points plotted on an x-y axis, the place on the
x-axis would be constant while that of the y-axis would vary widely.
The notes section of this text gathers the footnotes of the original:
all of the notes are included in some way and none are repeated.

If we read these pages and are convinced by them, we must
remind ourselves that the evidence of genocide was already clear in
December 2023, already a consensus of the human-rights community

less than three months after the attacks of October 7. South Africa's application to the ICJ feels now like a grim prelude to the enormous and interminable suffering still being inflicted upon Gaza, all with the full complicity of the United States and other governments arming Israel. Bombing and displacement. Starvation as a weapon of war. The murder of aid-seeking civilians. We have come to expect one or more of these in our daily news. The consensus that Israel is guilty of violating the Genocide Convention has only grown, and now includes, notably, Amnesty International and Human Rights Watch, each of whom issued a full report in December 2024; an independent commission of inquiry that presented a report on gender-based violence to the UN's Human Rights Council in March 2025; and the Israeli groups B'Tselem and Physicians for Human Rights–Israel, who issued reports in July 2025. At this writing a much-vaunted ceasefire agreement has brought little relief to Gaza, with Israel still engaging in routine military strikes, severely limiting aid, and obstructing efforts to clear debris and build shelter adequate for the coming winter months. Reporters without Borders has just issued its year-end findings: Israel is the clear world leader in murdering journalists, being responsible for 43% of such killings in the world, a significant increase from the 30% for which it was responsible in 2024. These attacks, often targeted, have been made futile by the dauntless reporting of Palestinians on the ground. Owing to their efforts, the ears of the world have heard the screams, and the eyes of the world have seen the starved infants. The conscience of the world has been moved, and the voices of the world will not be silent. We will bear witness to this genocide, now and for generations to come.

Feisal G. Mohamed, December 2025

CONTENTS

1   **Introduction**

16   **The Facts**

51   Genocidal Acts Committed against the Palestinian People
   1. Killing Palestinians in Gaza
   2. Causing serious bodily and mental harm to Palestinians in Gaza
   3. Mass expulsion from homes and displacement of Palestinians in Gaza
   4. Deprivation of access to adequate food and water to Palestinians in Gaza
   *5. Deprivation of access to adequate shelter, clothes, hygiene and sanitation
       to Palestinians in Gaza*
   6. Deprivation of adequate medical assistance to Palestinians in Gaza
   7. Destruction of Palestinian life in Gaza
   8. Imposing methods intended to prevent Palestinian births

144   Expressions of Genocidal Intent against the Palestinian
       People by Israeli State Officials and Others

162   Recognition of Israel's genocidal intent against Palestinians

168   **The Relief Sought**

180   **Notes**

INTRODUCTION

No

armed attack

can   provide any possible justification for   breaches

of the   Genocide Convention

No

armed attack					even an attack involving atrocity crimes

can		provide any possible justification for		breaches

of the		Genocide Convention

No

armed attack

can   provide any possible justification for   breaches

of the   Genocide Convention

as a matter of law

No

armed attack

can   provide any possible justification for   breaches

of the   Genocide Convention

as a matter of   morality

No

acts and omissions by Israel

are genocidal in character   intended to bring about the destruction of a substantial part

of the Palestinian national racial   ethnical group

killing Palestinians in Gaza

inflicting on them conditions of life calculated to bring about

their physical destruction   Israel

is committing genocide

and is continuing

acts of genocide inevitably form part of a continuum – as Raphaël Lemkin who coined the

term 'genocide' himself recognised

broader context   75-year-long apartheid   56-year-

long belligerent occupation of Palestinian territory   16-year-long blockade of Gaza

South Africa is also acutely aware

of its own obligation   to prevent genocide

the State of Palestine itself   has

called on "world leaders" to take responsibility   to stop the genocide against our people

apartheid expulsion ethnic cleansing annexation

occupation discrimination

genocide

genocidal acts against the Palestinian people in Gaza

killing them

genocidal intent

failure to provide or ensure essential food water medicine fuel shelter

for the besieged and blockaded Palestinian people   pushed   to the brink of

famine

herding them into ever smaller areas   in which they continue

to be attacked killed   harmed

waste to entire neighborhoods

agricultural land bakeries schools

universities businesses places of worship cemeteries cultural and archaeological sites municipal and

court buildings water and sanitation facilities and electricity

networks the Palestinian medical and healthcare system

continuing to reduce Gaza to rubble killing harming and destroying its people

Genocide

Genocide

urgent

genocide

extraordinary urgency

protect the Palestinian people in

Gaza

Genocide

Palestinian people in Gaza

genocide

Presidents of Algeria

Bolivia   Brazil Colombia Cuba Iran Türkiye   Venezuela have all described Israel's

actions as a genocide as has the Palestinian President   State officials and representatives from

Bangladesh Egypt Honduras Iraq Jordan Libya Malaysia Namibia Pakistan Syria

and Tunisia   referred to genocide or the risk thereof

Speaking on behalf of the 'Arab Group'

                                                                                    Egypt

      stated

          it is a collective punishment and *genocide against the Palestinian people*

                    an effort to eliminate the Palestinian people

Israel has been made fully aware

Israel has not responded

Israel denies

Israeli Prime Minister

asserted   "We are not stopping   We are continuing to fight   *we are deepening*

the fighting   this will be a long battle and it is not close to being over "

THE FACTS

the Gaza Strip

home to approximately 2.3 million people

almost half of them children

the Gaza Strip   one of the

most densely populated places in the world

                         subjected by Israel to   one of the

heaviest conventional bombing campaigns in the history of modern warfare

                                        more destruction than the razing of Syria's Aleppo

between 2012 and 2016   Ukraine's Mariupol   or proportionally   the Allied bombing in Germany in

World War II

the Gaza Strip

home to approximately 2.3 million people

almost half of them children   subjected by Israel to

6,000 bombs per week

Gaza is now a different colour

from space   a different texture

United Nations Secretary-General in a letter

dated 6 December 2023 to the President of the United Nations Security Council

"Civilians throughout Gaza face grave danger

Hospitals have turned into battlegrounds

Nowhere is safe in Gaza

potentially irreversible implications for Palestinians as

a whole   "

Entire multi-generational families have been wiped

out completely   more than 60 per cent of Gaza's housing

damaged or destroyed

Many fled the north of the territory to the south

having been ordered to do so by Israel only to be bombed again in the south no fully functioning hospital left in North Gaza

operations including amputations and

caesarean sections taking place without anaesthetic

Contagious and epidemic diseases are rife

The entire population in Gaza is at imminent risk of famine

silent slow deaths caused by hunger and

thirst   surpassing   violent deaths

disproportionate effect on children

Gaza

occupied by Israel

in 1967

80 per cent of Palestinians in Gaza are refugees   and their descendants

forced to flee during the mass displacement of

over 750,000 Palestinians or 'Nakba'   Nakba

features prominently in the history and consciousness

of Palestinians in Gaza as   for the wider Palestinian people

in 2005 Israel unilaterally 'disengaged' from Gaza

Notwithstanding   Israel continues to exercise control over   airspace territorial

waters land crossings water electricity electromagnetic sphere   civilian infrastructure .

                                                                                            near total

control exercised by Israel over access to Gaza   over its water fuel electricity   food supplies

has been demonstrated starkly since 7 October 2023

Israel imposed a stringent blockade of Gaza

following Hamas' electoral victory in 2006   declaring

the entire territory to be   hostile   restrictions

significantly tightened

prolonged   indefinite separation for many Palestinian families

Israel regulated food imports into Gaza in accordance with calories consumed per person to limit

the transfers of food to a 'humanitarian minimum'

Israel's   wide buffer zone inside Gaza's eastern border fence

impacts internal food

supply   reducing the main agricultural area for farming   fishing extremely

hazardous for Palestinians

naval blockade   policed by Israeli forces through the use of force   and the

confiscation of fishing equipment   severely reduced the fishing catchment area for Gaza's fishermen

to polluted waters immediately off the coastline

United Nations Special Rapporteur on the situation of human rights in the Palestinian territories

In 2022

he described the situation as follows

"In Gaza, the apparent strategy of Israel is the indefinite warehousing of an unwanted

population of 2 million Palestinians

collective punishment

a multi-decade process of dedevelopment and

deindustrialization

the hermetic sealing   of Gaza to the outside world

suffering was acknowledged by Antonio Guterres in May 2021 when he

stated "If there is a hell on earth it is the lives of the children of Gaza" "

the 'Great March of Return'   peaceful protest

along the separation fence between Gaza and Israel

the 'Great March of Return'   peaceful protest

along the separation fence between Gaza and Israel   thousands of Palestinians participated

every Friday for over 18 months demanding   the blockade imposed on Gaza be lifted and the

return of Palestinian refugees

the 'Great March of Return'   peaceful protest

along the separation fence between Gaza and Israel   thousands of Palestinians participated

every Friday for over 18 months demanding   the blockade imposed on Gaza be lifted and the

return of Palestinian refugees

Israeli soldiers   firing from behind the separation fence

the 'Great March of Return'   peaceful protest

along the separation fence between Gaza and Israel   thousands of Palestinians participated

every Friday for over 18 months

On one particularly lethal day

Israel killed 60 Palestinian protesters

Israeli soldiers firing from behind the separation fence

the 'Great March of Return'   peaceful protest

thousands of Palestinians participated

On one particularly lethal day

Israel killed 60 Palestinian protesters

Israeli soldiers firing from behind the separation fence

grounds to believe that Israeli snipers

intentionally shot children   intentionally shot health

workers   journalists

Israeli snipers shot disabled demonstrators intentionally

214 Palestinians

including 46 children were killed during the 'Great March of Return'   peaceful protest

along the separation fence between Gaza and Israel

On one particularly lethal day

Israel killed 60 Palestinian protesters

Israeli soldiers firing from behind the separation fence

maiming was not accidental   Israel permitted snipers to shoot at the

legs of the "major inciters"   One Israeli soldier admitted   he shot 42 knees in one day

(1 September 2008, Archbishop Desmond Tutu and Professor Christine Chinkin):

shelling on 8 November 2006 of Beit Hanoun took lives inflicted horrendous physical and mental injuries tore families apart destroyed homes took away livelihoods and traumatized a population

— Report of the United Nations Fact-Finding Mission on the Gaza Conflict established pursuant to Human Rights Council resolution S-9/1 of 12 January 2009 (25 September 2009):[119]

"36. . . . The Mission *did not find any evidence to support the allegations that hospital facilities were used by the Gaza authorities or by Palestinian armed groups* to shield military activities or that ambulances were used to transport combatants or for other military purposes. On the basis of its own investigations and the statements by United Nations officials, the Mission *excludes that Palestinian armed groups engaged in combat activities from United Nations facilities* that were used as shelters during the military operations. . . .

55. The Mission investigated four incidents in which the Israeli armed forces coerced Palestinian civilian men at gunpoint to take part in house searches during the military operations. . . . The Mission concludes that this practice amounts to *the use of Palestinian civilians as human shields* and is therefore prohibited by international humanitarian law. . . . The Palestinian men used as human shields were *questioned under threat of death or injury* to extract information about Hamas, Palestinian combatants and tunnels. This constitutes a further violation of international humanitarian law. . . .

60. In addition to arbitrary deprivation of liberty and violation of due process rights, the cases of the detained Palestinian civilians highlight a common thread of the interaction between Israeli soldiers and Palestinian civilians which also emerged clearly in many cases discussed elsewhere in the report: *continuous and systematic abuse, outrages on personal dignity, humiliating and degrading treatment* contrary to fundamental principles of international humanitarian law and human rights law. The Mission concludes that this treatment constitutes the *infliction of a collective penalty on these civilians and amounts to measures of intimidation and terror.* . . .

382. In assessing the Israeli strikes against the Legislative Council building and the main prison, the Mission first of all notes that Hamas is an organization with distinct political, military and social welfare components. . . .

391. The Mission rejects the analysis of present and former senior Israeli officials that, because of the alleged nature of the Hamas government in Gaza, the distinction between civilian and military parts of the government infrastructure is no longer relevant in relation to Israel's conflict with Hamas. . . .

392. The Mission is of the view that *this is a dangerous argument that should be vigorously rejected as incompatible with the cardinal principle of distinction.* International humanitarian law prohibits attacks against targets that do not make an effective contribution to military action. Attacks that are not directed against military (or dual use) objectives are violations of the laws of war, no matter how promising the attacker considers them from a strategic or political point of view. . . .

522. The warning to go to city centres came at the start of the ground invasion. In the Mission's view it was unreasonable to assume, in the circumstances, that civilians would indeed leave their homes. As a consequence, *the conclusion that allegedly formed part of the logic of soldiers on the ground that those who had stayed put had to be combatants was wholly unwarranted.* . . .

629. Taking into account the weapons used, and in particular the use of white phosphorous in and around *a hospital that the Israeli armed forces knew was not only dealing with scores of injured and wounded but also giving shelter to several hundred civilians*, the Mission finds, based on all the information available to it, that in directly striking the hospital and the ambulance depot the Israeli armed forces in these circumstances violated article 18 of the Fourth Geneva Convention and violated customary international law in relation to proportionality. . . .

1027. The Mission . . . found that the systematic destruction of food, production, water services and construction industries was related to the *overall policy of disproportionate destruction of a significant part of Gaza's infrastructure.*

1214. Through its overly broad framing of the "supporting infrastructure", the Israeli armed forces have sought to construct a scope for their activities that, in the Mission's view, was *designed to have inevitably dire consequences for the non-combatants in Gaza* . . . .

1215. Statements by political and military leaders prior to and during the military operations in Gaza leave little doubt that disproportionate destruction and violence against civilians were part of a deliberate policy. . . .

1883. The Gaza military operations were, according to the Israeli Government, thoroughly and extensively planned. *While the Israeli Government has sought to portray its operations as essentially a response to rocket attacks in the exercise of its right to self-defence, the Mission considers the plan to have been directed, at least in part, at a different target: the people of Gaza as a whole.* . . .

1888. The Mission recognizes fully that the Israeli armed forces, like any army attempting to act within the parameters of international law, must avoid taking undue risks with their soldiers' lives, but neither can they transfer that risk onto the lives of civilian men, women and children. The fundamental principles of distinction and proportionality apply on the battlefield, whether that battlefield is a built-up urban area or an open field.

1889. The *repeated failure to distinguish between combatants and civilians appears to the Mission to have been the result of deliberate guidance issued to soldiers*, as described by some of them, and not the result of occasional lapses. . . .

1891. It is clear from evidence gathered by the Mission that the destruction of food supply installations, water sanitation systems, concrete factories and residential houses was the result of a *deliberate and systematic policy* by the Israeli armed forces. *It was not carried out because those objects presented a military threat or opportunity, but to make the daily process of living, and dignified living, more difficult for the civilian population.* . . .

1892. Allied to the *systematic destruction of the economic capacity of the Gaza Strip, there appears also to have been an assault on the dignity of the people.* This was seen not only in the use of human shields and unlawful detentions sometimes in unacceptable conditions, but also in the vandalizing of houses when occupied and the way in which people were treated when their houses were entered. The graffiti on the walls, the obscenities and often racist slogans, *all constituted an overall image of humiliation and dehumanization of the Palestinian population.* . . .

1893. The operations were carefully planned in all their phases. Legal opinions and advice were given throughout the planning stages and at certain operational levels during the campaign. There were almost no mistakes made according to the Government of Israel.

—Report of the detailed findings of the independent commission of inquiry established pursuant to Human Rights Council resolution S-21/1 of 23 July 2014 (24 June 2015):

shells fired   dropping of over 100 one-

ton bombs

artillery barrage

indiscriminate attacks

The choice of the methods and means used by the IDF cannot be reconciled with the obligation to take constant care to spare civilians and civilian objects

commander of the Brigade responsible for the Khuza'a operation

"Palestinians have to understand that this does not pay off"

The West Bank (including East Jerusalem)

                                        is geographically separated

from Gaza   fragmented by Israeli settlements

Area A

Area B

Area C

the number of Israeli settlers transferred into the West Bank (including East Jerusalem) has increased dramatically from an estimated 247,000 at the time of the Oslo Accords   to over 700,000 in 2023

Much of the West Bank is off-limits to Palestinians

Access to   natural resources   especially   water disproportionately allocated to   settlers

housing and commercial development

deeply discriminatory

ongoing land

confiscation   home demolitions   denial of building permits

forcible transfer of Palestinians

confiscating land for settlements   military weapons training areas and other

uses exclusive to the occupying power

East Jerusalem   increasingly detached   from its traditional

national   economic   cultural and family connections with the West Bank because of the wall

growing ring of settlements and related checkpoints   discriminatory permit regime

East Jerusalem

West Bank   wall

settlements   checkpoints

an apartheid regime

discriminatory land zoning

punitive and administrative house demolitions   Israeli army incursions into Palestinian

villages towns cities refugee camps   routine violent Israeli raids on

homes arbitrary arrests   indefinitely renewable administrative detention

Palestinians

without basic protections

Israeli settlers

with full due process

Save the Children

                  children   killed

            children have been killed by Israeli soldiers and settlers

    children wounded

a wave of arbitrary mass arrests   has detained more than 3,000 Palestinians

including for social media posts relating to the situation in Gaza

19

Israeli prison guards were reportedly questioned for beating to death one of the prisoners   Tha'er Abu

Asab   in Ketziot Prison

Tha'er Abu

Asab

Since 7 October 2023

There have been 236 attacks on healthcare   including hospitals   in the West Bank with Israeli forces detaining health staff and ambulances

extreme

Israeli settler violence   alongside punitive or administrative house demolitions carried out by   Israeli army and damage caused to homes during Israeli military raids

Israel's actions in the West Bank since 7 October 2023

including the driving out of vulnerable Palestinian communities from their lands

intrinsically connected to Israel's actions in Gaza   at the very least important context to

Israel's violations of the Genocide Convention

the military wing of Hamas   and Palestinian Islamic Jihad   launched a large barrage of rockets towards Israel

attacked Israeli military bases and civilian towns   as well as a music festival attended by thousands of young people

South Africa unequivocally condemns the targeting of Israeli and foreign national civilians   and the taking of hostages on 7 October 2023

over 1,200 Israelis and foreign nationals have been killed in Israel

including 36 children

Approximately 240 civilians   elderly people   women   children and Israeli soldiers were taken as hostages into Gaza

57 hostages are reported to have been killed in Israeli

bombardments of Gaza   a further three hostages   shot dead by Israeli soldiers

in Gaza

Genocidal Acts Committed against the Palestinian People

Israel is deliberately imposing telecommunications blackouts on Gaza and

restricting access by fact-finding bodies   and the international media   Palestinian

journalists are being killed

In the two months since 7 October 2023 the number of journalists killed already exceeded that

of the entirety of World War II

Humanitarian veterans who have served in war zones and disasters around the world   people who

have seen everything   say they have seen nothing like what they see today in Gaza a moral failure   intolerable suffering

an apocalyptic situation

                                                            utter   deepening

horror

       living hell   everything is unprecedented   out of

words to describe what is going on

1. Killing Palestinians in Gaza

Over 21,110   killed

                            7,780 people

                 presumed dead under the rubble   dying slow

deaths   or decomposing in the streets where they were killed

                 bodies are being buried in mass graves   often unidentified

Nowhere is safe in Gaza

Palestinians in Gaza have

been killed in their homes   in places where they sought shelter   in hospitals   in UNRWA schools   in

churches   in mosques   as they tried to find food and water for their families   They have been killed

if they failed to evacuate in the places to which they fled   and even while they attempted to flee along

Israeli declared "safe routes"

Israeli soldiers performing summary

executions   including of multiple members of the same family   men   women   older people

execution in Gaza City of at least 11 male members of the Annan family

boys and men   shot in front

of their family   before the women and children were then attacked hundreds of multigenerational families have been killed

in their entirety   mothers fathers children siblings grandparents aunts

cousins   often all killed together

medics in Gaza have had to coin a new acronym

'WCNSF'   'wounded child no surviving family'

Palestinian children

killed

killed every day   killed

children killed

Gaza is

a graveyard for children

prompted UNICEF's spokesperson to call Israel's attacks on Gaza a

"war on children"

Doctors journalists teachers academics   killed

Israel has killed   over 311 doctors   nurses and other health workers

103 journalists   over one per

day

over 209 teachers and educational staff   144 United Nations employees have

been killed

it will take years to recover the remains of people from beneath the rubble

2. Causing serious bodily and mental harm to Palestinians in Gaza

Burns and amputations are typical

injuries   an estimated 1,000 children having lost one or both legs   Israeli

forces using white phosphorous in densely populated areas

                                        can cause deep and severe burns   penetrating even

through bone

severe mental

trauma in the Palestinian population

tens of thousands of Palestinian children   have lost at least one parent

r epeated exposure to conflict and violence

high levels of psychological distress

disruption of access to education

lifelong effects on   physical and mental

health

                                        Emergency Coordinator for

Médecins sans Frontières interviewed on her return from five weeks in Gaza

          " I t's even worse in reality than it looks   It's   the amount of suffering is just something

          incomparable   unbearable   I'm speechless

                    generations of children   will be handicapped   will be traumatized

          children in our mental health program   telling us that they would rather die than

continue living in Gaza now "

Palestinians in Gaza

        arrested blindfolded forced to undress and remain outside in

the cold weather   forced on to trucks and taken to unknown locations   Medics and first

responders   repeatedly detained

incommunicado at unknown locations

Videos published by Israeli media on Christmas Day appeared

to show hundreds of Palestinians   rounded up inside Al Yarmouk football stadium in Gaza City

including children   older people   persons with disabilities   forced to strip to their underwear

in degrading conditions

Images of mutilated and

burned corpses

billed as 'exclusive content

from the Gaza Strip'

circulated in Israel via

Telegram channel called

'72 Virgins – Uncensored'

3. Mass expulsion from homes and displacement of Palestinians in Gaza

approximately 85 per cent of the population   forced from their homes

nowhere safe   to flee

Israel   issuing 'evacuation orders'

                                        The first such order

demanded that   1.1 million Palestinians

        move to the South of Gaza within a 24-hour window

                                                tantamount to a death sentence   for

hospital patients

Palestinians fleeing the North pursuant to Israel's evacuation orders were urged to move south

Israeli forces

continued bombing south

killing many Palestinians who evacuated   prompting many

Palestinian families   to return north to   be   bombed in the familiar surrounding of

their homes

fleeing the North   move south

                                                        bombing south

            return north   bombed

Israel   dropping leaflets urging Palestinians to leave areas in the South to which they had

previously been told to flee

forcibly displaced again

Israel   published a detailed map online dividing the Gaza Strip into hundreds

of small areas   to provide notice of Israeli orders to evacuate

                    ahead of planned air strikes   the publication does not

specify where people should evacuate to   after months of bombardment

                    most Palestinians in Gaza have

            no reliable way of accessing the map

"the people of Gaza are being told to move like human pinballs   ricocheting between

ever-smaller slivers of the south without any of the basics for survival "

Palestinians are not safe   even in those   small   slivers

No place is safe   there is nowhere safe to go

increased population density as a result

of the evacuation 'orders' is also rendering Israeli strikes ever more lethal   On Christmas Eve   the

Israeli army bombed Al Maghazi Refugee Camp   to which tens of

thousands of Palestinians had fled from the North   killing an estimated 86 people   including many

women and children   injuring many others

forced evacuation   is necessarily permanent Israel

has now damaged or destroyed   60 per cent of

the entire housing stock in Gaza   the North of Gaza

largely unlivable   the South reaching a similar level

repeating a long history of mass forced displacement of Palestinians by

Israel

The forced displacements in Gaza are genocidal

calculated to bring about the physical destruction of Palestinians in Gaza

4. Deprivation of access to adequate food and water to Palestinians in Gaza

complete siege   no electricity no

food   no water   no fuel

conditions for the effective delivery of humanitarian aid no longer exist

Shelves are empty   wallets are empty

stomachs are empty   one bakery is operating in the whole of Gaza

the Secretary-General was clear to advise that focusing on the

number of trucks permitted into Gaza daily was misleading

"

This is a mistake   The real problem is that *the way Israel is*

conducting this offensive is creating massive obstacles to the distribution of humanitarian aid

inside Gaza "

Israel has   pushed   Gaza to the brink of famine

                                                            Gaza   *starving*

levels of starvation rising daily   h unger is ravaging

Gaza   f our out of five of the hungriest people

anywhere in the world are in Gaza

                                                                        d esperate

hungry   terrified people

World Health Organization

Emergency Medical

Teams Coordinator   "Everywhere we go

people are asking us for food even in the hospital   I walked around in the emergency department

somebody with an open bleeding wound an open fracture they asked for food If that's not an indicator

of   desperation   I don't know what is"

Israel's continuing strikes on Gaza

on   bakeries   water facilities and last remaining operating mill   razing   agricultural

lands crops orchards   food infrastructure in Gaza

no longer functional

Bread is scarce or non-existent

Many

Palestinians   collecting spilled flour from aid distributions from

the road

lack of water is severely impacting lactating women   who

                              require a supply of 7.5 litres of water a day for drinking   sanitation

and hygiene   Young mothers

                                        forced to use contaminated water

to prepare formula   where it is available

chronic unavailability of formula   risking the lives of newborn babies   already

dying from avoidable causes

Israeli plans to flood tunnels in Gaza with seawater

risks   further degradation and collapse of Gaza's water and sewage

infrastructure   long-lasting contamination of Gaza's aquifer and soil

risks causing an ecological catastrophe   would leave Gaza with no

drinkable water devastate what little agriculture is possible

The United Nations Special Rapporteur for the right to water is reported to have compared

the plan to the mythical Roman 'salting' of the fields of Carthage

more Palestinians in Gaza may die from starvation and disease

than airstrikes

than airstrikes

more Palestinians in Gaza may die from starvation and disease

than airstrikes

more Palestinians in Gaza may die from starvation and disease

than airstrikes

more Palestinians in Gaza may die from starvation and disease

than airstrikes

more Palestinians in Gaza may die from starvation and disease

than airstrikes

more Palestinians in Gaza may die from starvation and disease

than airstrikes

more Palestinians in Gaza may die from starvation and disease

than airstrikes

more Palestinians in Gaza may die from starvation and disease

than airstrikes

more Palestinians in Gaza may die from starvation and disease

than airstrikes

5. Deprivation of access to adequate shelter, clothes, hygiene and sanitation to Palestinians in Gaza

71.   The majority of the 1.9 million displaced Palestinians in Gaza are seeking shelter in UNRWA facilities, which primarily consist of schools and tents.[310] These locations are themselves not safe: to date — and despite Israel having been provided with the coordinates of all United Nations facilities[311] — Israel has killed hundreds of Palestinian men, women and children seeking shelter in UNRWA facilities, and injured over a thousand.[312]

72.   The situation in UNRWA shelters was described as follows by the Commissioner-General of UNRWA in his 7 December 2023 letter of which the United Nations General Assembly took note in its Resolution ES-10/22 of 12 December 2023:

> "Today, as a result of Israel's military operation, nearly 1.2 million civilians are sheltering in UNRWA premises. The Agency has become the primary *platform for humanitarian assistance to over 2.2 million people in Gaza — a platform on the verge of collapse.*
>
> UNRWA is, as of today, still operational in Gaza, though just barely. Our staff are still operating health centers, managing shelters, and supporting traumatized people, some arriving carrying their dead children. We are still distributing food, even though the corridors and courtyards of our premises are too crowded to walk through. Our staff take their children to work so they know they are safe or can die together. *More than 130 UNRWA staff are confirmed killed in bombardments, most with their families*; the number might rise by the time you read this. At least 70% of UNRWA staff are displaced, and lack food, water and adequate shelter. We are hanging on by our fingertips. If UNRWA collapses, humanitarian assistance in Gaza will also collapse.
>
> *The humanitarian situation is now untenable.* Conditions in Gaza were already appalling when I stayed overnight two weeks ago. I witnessed constant explosive munitions from sky, land and sea, and the massive destruction of civilian infrastructure.
>
> This week, the Israeli military forces have instructed people to move further South, forcing Gaza's population into an ever-shrinking space. Shelters are shockingly overcrowded, with high risk of epidemic illness. In these overfull and unsanitary spaces, more than 700 people use a single toilet, women give birth (an average of 25 per day), and people nurse open wounds. Tens of thousands sleep in courtyards and streets. People burn plastic to stay warm. Nearly 90 UNRWA premises, including schools, have been hit or impacted by munitions, killing over 270 internally displaced people, many this week. In Gaza as a whole, over 16,000 people, two thirds of whom are women and children, are reported killed during bombardments. Large swathes of Gaza are destroyed and uninhabitable.
>
> *The premise of UNRWA's mandate — to provide services to Palestine Refugees until there is a political solution — is at great risk:* without safe shelter and aid, civilians in Gaza risk death or will be forced to Egypt and beyond. Forced displacement out of Gaza may end prospects for the political solution that is intrinsic to UNRWA's mandate, with grave risks for regional peace and security. A forced displacement beyond Palestinian land, reminiscent of the 1948 Nakba, must be prevented.
>
> In my 35 years working in complex emergencies, *I have never written such a letter — predicting the killing of my staff and the collapse of the mandate I am expected to fulfil.*"[313]

Al-Mawasi

along the Mediterranean Sea

safe zone

Al-Mawasi   a sandy barren strip of

approximately 14 square kilometers along the Mediterranean Sea without   water food

or sanitation   so-called 'safe zone' to which Israel has told Palestinians in Gaza to flee is anything

but safe   Nowhere

in Gaza is safe

There is no access to clean water there are

crumbling sanitation facilities   children starving in the so-called 'safe zone' of Al-

Mawasi

‘safe zone’

safe   Nowhere

in Gaza is safe

                                               no

                                                            ‘safe zone’

6. *Deprivation of adequate medical assistance to Palestinians in Gaza*

w e have descended into depths from which we must quickly

emerge

Israel has declared

an unrelenting war on the health system in Gaza

healthcare infrastructure in the Gaza strip has been completely obliterated

a shameful war on healthcare workers

depths from which we must quickly

emerge

In a letter to the United Nations Security Council on 4 December 2023   the International

President of Médecins Sans Frontières wrote

We are watching as *hospitals are turned into morgues and ruins*

                              shot at by tanks and guns encircled and raided killing

patients and medical staff

                                        They have had to

amputate limbs from children suffering from severe burns without anaesthesia or sterilised

surgical tools   some doctors have had to leave

patients behind after facing the unimaginable choice between their lives or those of their

patients

Four of our MSF staff have been killed   many more have lost family members

Northern Gaza is being erased from the map

                        strikes are also hitting overcrowded squalid refugee camps

                                        If the bombs do not get them

infectious diseases and starvation will

"We did what we could   Remember us " These are the words   Dr Mahmoud Abu Nujaila

who has since been killed in a hospital strike   wrote on a Gaza hospital whiteboard normally

used for planning surgeries

"We did what we could   "

                                When the guns fall silent and the true scale of devastation is

revealed will the Council and its members be able to say the same?

"We did what we could   Remember us "   Dr Mahmoud Abu Nujaila

Palestinian hospitals

death zone s   scenes of bloodbath   devastation

despair

some of Gaza's most experienced and skilled doctors   Dr Hani

Al Haitham Head of the Emergency Section at Al Shifa Hospital   Dr Sameera

Ghirafi   Dr Mohammed Dabbour Head of Pathology at Al Shifa Hospital

Dr Medhat Saidam

plastic reconstructive burn surgeon at Al Shifa Hospital   Dr Hammam Alloh nephrologist at Al

Shifa Hospital

Those killed include some of Gaza's most experienced and skilled doctors including Dr Hani Al Haitham   Head of the Emergency Section at Al Shifa Hospital   killed with his wife   Dr Sameera Ghirafi and their children   Dr Mohammed Dabbour Head of Pathology at Al Shifa Hospital reportedly killed with his son and father while attempting to flee Gaza City   Dr Medhat Saidam plastic reconstructive burn surgeon at Al Shifa Hospital and Dr Hammam Alloh nephrologist at Al Shifa Hospital were killed in attacks on their family homes   Interviewed shortly before his death Dr Alloh responded as follows when asked why he was not fleeing the North to the South "If I go who would treat my patients? We are not animals we have the right to proper health care   You think I went to medical school and for my postgraduate degrees for a total of 14 years so I think only about my life and not my patients?"

Hani

killed with his wife   Sameera

and their children

Mohammed

killed with his son and father

Medhat

and   Hammam

killed in attacks on their family homes

                                        Even those

tending to and counting the dead   Saeed Al Shorbaji Director of Nasser Hospital's mortuary

have themselves been killed

Dina Abu Mohsen

12-

year old Dina Abu Mohsen

year old Dina Abu Mohsen   interviewed by UNICEF

year old Dina Abu Mohsen   interviewed by UNICEF after losing her parents

year old Dina Abu Mohsen   interviewed by UNICEF after losing her parents two siblings and her

leg in an Israeli strike on her home

year old Dina Abu Mohsen   interviewed by UNICEF after losing her parents two siblings and her

leg in an Israeli strike on her home   was then killed herself when the Israeli army shelled the

hospital where she was being treated

Palestinians have died as a direct result of Israel cutting off electricity and fuel to

hospitals they include five premature babies and 40 ICU and kidney patients at Al Shifa hospital

Palestinians have died as a direct result of Israel's forced evacuation of hospitals   including at

least four babies in Al Nasr hospital whose tiny bodies were found weeks later

decomposing in their hospital beds

mass grave

    Hossam Abu Safiya

  stated "

       I have never seen such a thing before"

Israeli bulldozers excavated and exhumed a hospital

mass grave in the besieged Kamal Adwan hospital on 16 December   where 26 Palestinians had been

buried   Hossam Abu Safiya   Head of Pediatric Services

stated   " t he soldiers dug up the graves this morning and dragged the bodies with bulldozers

then crushed the bodies with the bulldozers   I have never seen such a thing before"

soldiers dug up the graves   dragged the bodies with bulldozers

then crushed the bodies with the bulldozers

a boy from the North   leg   blown off   spent three

or four days trying to reach the south delayed by checkpoints   smell of decomposition was

clear   that boy had shrapnel all over

                                a woman with shrapnel injuries in her abdomen   walked

from the North to the South pressing a towel against her wounds

                                                                Palestinians

                        in a forced march   North   South

        South onwards   dragging hospital beds behind cars

scenes from a horror movie

caesareans without anaesthetic

unclean

wounds   infested with worms and flies   infected necrotic gangrenous

One doctor described having to do procedures without anesthetic he said

"I was forced to do dressing changes on massive wounds excruciatingly painful wounds There was a girl with just her whole body covered in shrapnel   She was nine I ended up having to change and clean these wounds with no anaesthetic and no analgesic I managed to find some intravenous paracetamol to give her   her Dad was crying I was crying   the poor child was screaming   "

the death toll from disease and hunger   could be multiples of that from

fighting and air strikes

7. Destruction of Palestinian life in Gaza

On 16 November 2023   15 United Nations Special Rapporteurs and 21 members of the United

Nations Working Groups   warning of a "genocide in the making" in Gaza   observed   the level of

destruction   of housing units   hospitals   schools   mosques

bakeries   water pipes   sewage and electricity networks   threatens to make the continuation of

Palestinian life in Gaza impossible

Israel has destroyed

entire streets   entire neighbourhoods

everything that once sustained Palestinian life

Israel has destroyed

entire streets   entire neighbourhoods

Shuja'iyya a suburb of Gaza City once home to approximately 110,000 Palestinians

now   a vast wasteland entirely flattened   Its shops schools vibrant

market place family homes doctors clinics historic streets   Ibn Uthman Mosque

everything that once sustained Palestinian life   damaged or destroyed

Other areas in Gaza   similar   destruction

Beit Hanoun   Beit Lahia   Gaza Old City   Al Rimal   Nuseirat refugee camp

Israel has targeted the Palace of Justice   the main Palestinian court building in

Gaza   housing the Palestinian Supreme Court   Constitutional Court   Court of Appeal

Court of First Instance   Administrative Court   Magistrates' Court

Israel has also significantly damaged the Palestinian Legislative

Council complex

Israel

has targeted Gaza City's Central Archive building   containing thousands of

historical documents and national records   an essential

archive of Palestinian history

Israel has left Gaza City's main public library in ruins   It has also damaged or destroyed

countless bookshops publishing houses libraries   hundreds of educational facilities

Israel has

targeted every one of Gaza's four universities

 Suffian Tayeh   President of the Islamic University   an award-winning physicist and UNESCO Chair of Astronomy Astrophysics and Space Sciences

Dr Ahmed Hamdi Abo Asa Dean of the Software Engineering Department at the University of Palestine

Professor Muhammad Eid Shabir Professor of Immunology and Virology   former President of the Islamic University of Gaza   Professor Refaat Alareer poet and Professor of Comparative Literature and Creative Writing at the Islamic University of Gaza

Professor Alareer was a co-founder of 'We Are Not Numbers'   a Palestinian youth project seeking to tell the stories behind otherwise impersonal accounts of Palestinians   and Palestinian deaths   in the news

Israel has damaged and destroyed numerous centres of Palestinian learning and culture including Al Zafar Dmari Mosque and Center for Manuscripts and Ancient Documents the Orthodox Cultural Centre the Al Qarara Cultural Museum the Gaza Centre for Culture and Arts the Arab Social Cultural Centre the Hakawi Society for Culture and Arts the Rafah Museum – Gaza's newly opened museum of Palestinian heritage housing hundreds of cultural and archaeological artefacts Israel's attacks have destroyed Gaza's ancient history eight sites damaged or destroyed including the ancient port of Gaza (known as 'Anthedon Harbour' or 'Al Balakhiya') the archaeological site of a 2,000-year-old Roman cemetery listed on both the Islamic Heritage List and the tentative UNESCO World Heritage List Israel has also destroyed Gaza City's 'Old City' its historic houses mosques churches markets schools also destroyed Gaza's more recent history of more hopeful times including the Rashad al-Shawa Cultural Center – site of a historic meeting between Bill Clinton and Yasser Arafat 25 years ago

Israel is destroying Gaza's future academic and cultural potential

Israel has damaged or destroyed an estimated 318 Muslim and Christian religious sites

These include the Great

Omari Mosque   originally a fifth century Byzantine church   iconic landmark of Gaza's history

architecture   cultural heritage   a place of worship by Christians and Muslims for over 1,000

years

Israeli shelling   damaged the Church of Saint Porphyrius   founded in 425 AD

believed to be the third oldest church in the world

Israel has sought to destroy

Israel has killed

and is killing Palestinian story-tellers and poets   farmers and fishermen

local legends   pastry chef Masoud Muhammad al-Qatati killed in an Israeli airstrike on his house on 3

November 2023   whose shop's motto was 'let the poor eat'   reputation for giving away

knafeh   to indigent customers   earned him the nickname 'Father of the Poor'

year-old Elham Farah   from one of Palestine's oldest Christian families   accordionist and

music teacher   known as 'Mother Orange' to generations of Palestinian music students for her shock of

red hair   shot dead by an Israeli sniper outside the Holy Family Church in Gaza City when she

returned home for warm clothes   left to bleed to death

Al-Shaima Saidam   the student

with the highest final high school exam grades in the whole of Palestine   killed with multiple members

of her family in a strike on Al Nuseirat refugee camp

Israel is

bombing

and bulldozing graveyards   destroying family records   photographs   wiping out entire multi-

generational families   killing maiming   traumatising a generation of children

8. Imposing measures intended to prevent Palestinian births

70 percent of those killed estimated to be women and children

Two mothers

are estimated to be killed every hour in Gaza

multiple eye-witness accounts of pregnant women

being killed by Israeli soldiers   including while trying to access healthcare

5,500

pregnant Palestinian women in Gaza giving birth each month   in unsafe conditions

often with no clean water   in shelters   in their homes   in the streets

in overwhelmed healthcare facilities

                                                                doctors

compelled to perform ordinarily unnecessary hysterectomies on young women

        leaving them unable to have more children

                                the only option facing Palestinian women in Gaza who 'bleed

out' after giving birth is to undergo a hysterectomy

Premature births have   increased by between 25-30 per cent   stressed and

traumatised pregnant women   compelled to walk long

distances in search of safety   attempting to escape from bombs   crowded into shelters in often

squalid conditions

                                                            newborns up to three months old are dying of

diarrhoea hypothermia and other preventable causes

premature and underweight babies have little to no chance of survival

November 2023 the United Nations Special Rapporteur on violence against women and girls

expressly warned that

" T he reproductive violence inflicted by Israel on Palestinian women   newborn babies   infants

and children could be qualified as   *acts of genocide*

States must prevent and punish such acts in accordance with their

responsibilities under the Genocide Convention "

The forced displacements in Gaza are genocidal in that they are taking place in circumstances calculated to bring about the physical destruction of Palestinians in Gaza It is clear that Israel is through its actions and policies in Gaza deliberately inflicting on Palestinians conditions of life calculated to bring about their destruction These conditions deliberately inflicted by Israel are calculated to bring about the destruction of the Palestinian group in Gaza Israel is through its relentless attacks on the Palestinian healthcare system deliberately inflicting on Palestinians in Gaza conditions of life calculated to bring about their destruction Israel is thereby deliberately inflicting on the Palestinian group in Gaza conditions of life calculated to bring about its destruction The forced displacements in Gaza are genocidal in that they are taking place in circumstances calculated to bring about the physical destruction of Palestinians in Gaza It is clear that Israel is through its actions and policies in Gaza deliberately inflicting on Palestinians conditions of life calculated to bring about their destruction These conditions deliberately inflicted by Israel are calculated to bring about the destruction of the Palestinian group in Gaza Israel is through its relentless attacks on the Palestinian healthcare system deliberately inflicting on Palestinians in Gaza conditions of life calculated to bring about their destruction Israel is thereby deliberately inflicting on the Palestinian group in Gaza conditions of life calculated to bring about its destruction The forced displacements in Gaza are genocidal in that they are taking place in circumstances calculated to bring about the physical destruction of Palestinians in Gaza It is clear that Israel is through its actions and policies in Gaza deliberately inflicting

The forced displacements in Gaza are genocidal in that they are taking place in circumstances calculated to bring about the physical destruction of Palestinians in Gaza It is clear that Israel is through its actions and policies in Gaza deliberately inflicting on Palestinians conditions of life calculated to bring about their destruction as a Palestinian group

Expressions of Genocidal Intent against the Palestinian People by Israeli State Officials and Others

Israeli State officials' specific intent   to commit and persist in

committing genocidal acts   significant and overt since October 2023

statements of intent   combined with the level of killing maiming displacement and

destruction on the ground together with the siege   evidence an unfolding and continuing genocide

Prime Minister of Israel:

Prime Minister Benjamin Netanyahu

On 16 October 2023 in a formal address to the

Israeli Knesset   described the situation as "a struggle between the children of light and the

children of darkness between humanity and the law of the jungle"

a dehumanising theme to

which he returned   on 3 November 2023 in a letter to Israeli

soldiers and officers also published on the platform 'X'

" t his is the war between the sons of light and the sons of darkness

the good will defeat the extreme evil that

threatens us and the entire world "

also returned to the theme in

his 'Christmas message'   "we're facing monsters monsters who murdered children in

front of their parents   This is a battle not only of Israel against these barbarians it's a battle

of civilization against barbarism"

Amalek

Amalek

relevant biblical passage reads

as follows   "Now go attack Amalek and proscribe all that belongs to him   Spare no one but

kill alike men and women infants and sucklings oxen and sheep camels and asses"

On 28 October 2023 as Israeli forces prepared their land

invasion of Gaza the Prime Minister invoked the Biblical story of

Amalek   "you must remember what Amalek has done to you says our

Holy Bible And we do remember"   The Prime Minister referred again to Amalek in the letter

sent on 3 November 2023 to Israeli soldiers and officers

President of Israel: On 12 October 2023 President Isaac Herzog

"It's

an entire nation out there that's responsible It's not true this rhetoric about civilians not aware

not involved It's absolutely not true   we will fight until we break their backbone "

Israeli Minister of Defence: On 9 October 2023 Defence Minister Yoav Gallant

advised that Israel was "imposing a complete siege on Gaza No

electricity no food no water no fuel Everything is closed We are fighting human animals and

we are acting accordingly "

informed troops on the Gaza border that he had "released

all the restraints"

"Gaza won't return to what it was before We will

eliminate everything If it doesn't take one day it will take a week It will take weeks or even

months we will reach all places "

—   **Israeli Minister for National Security**: On 10 November 2023, Itamar Ben-Gvir clarified the government's position in a televised address, stating: "[t]o be clear, when we say that Hamas should be destroyed, it also means those who celebrate, those who support, and those who hand out candy — they're all terrorists, and they should also be destroyed."[456]

—   **Israeli Minister of Energy and Infrastructure**: 'Tweeting' on 13 October 2023, Israel Katz stated: "All the civilian population in Gaza is ordered to leave immediately. We will win. They will not receive a drop of water or a single battery until they leave the world."[457] On 12 October 2023, he 'tweeted': "Humanitarian aid to Gaza? No electrical switch will be turned on, no water hydrant will be opened and no fuel truck will enter until the Israeli abductees are returned home. Humanitarianism for humanitarianism. And no one will preach us morality."[458]

—   **Israeli Minister of Finance**: On 8 October 2023, Bezalel Smotrich stated at a meeting of the Israeli Cabinet that "[w]e need to deal a blow that hasn't been seen in 50 years and take down Gaza."[459]

—   **Israeli Minister of Heritage**: On 1 November 2023, Amichai Eliyahu posted on Facebook: "The north of the Gaza Strip, more beautiful than ever. Everything is blown up and flattened, simply a pleasure for the eyes … We must talk about the day after. In my mind, we will hand over lots to all those who fought for Gaza over the years and to those evicted from Gush Katif" [a former Israeli settlement].[460] He later argued against humanitarian aid as "[w]e wouldn't hand the Nazis humanitarian aid", and "there is no such thing as uninvolved civilians in Gaza".[461] He also posited a nuclear attack on the Gaza Strip.[462]

—   **Israeli Minister of Agriculture**: On 11 November 2023, Avi Dichter in a television interview recalled the Nakba of 1948, in which over 80 percent of the Palestinian population of the new Israeli State was forced from or fled their homes, stating that "[w]e are now actually rolling out the Gaza Nakba".[463]

—   **Deputy Speaker of the Knesset and Member of the Foreign Affairs and Security Committee**: On 7 October 2023, Nissim Vaturi 'tweeted' that: "[n]ow we all have one common goal — erasing the Gaza Strip from the face of the earth. Those who are unable will be replaced."[464]

102.   Similar statements have been made by Israeli army officials, advisers and spokespersons, and others engaging with Israeli troops being deployed in Gaza:

—   **Israeli Army Coordinator of Government Activities in the Territories ('COGAT')**: On 9 October 2023, in a video statement addressed to Hamas and Gaza residents, published by COGAT's official channel, Major General Ghassan Alian warned: "Hamas became ISIS and the citizens of Gaza are celebrating instead of being horrified. Human animals are dealt with accordingly. Israel has imposed a total blockade on Gaza, no electricity, no water, just damage. You wanted hell, you will get hell."[465]

—   **Israeli Army Reservist Major General, former Head of the Israeli National Security Council, and adviser to the Defence Minister**:[466] On 7 October 2023, Giora Eiland, describing the Israeli order to cut off water and electricity to Gaza, wrote in an online journal: "This is what Israel has begun to do — we cut the supply of energy, water and diesel to the Strip . . . But it's not enough. In order to make the siege effective, we have to prevent others from giving assistance to Gaza . . . *The people should be told that they have two choices; to stay and to starve, or to leave.* If Egypt and other countries prefer that these people will perish in Gaza, this is their choice."[467] On the same day, he asserted in a national newspaper that "[w]hen you are at war with another country you don't feed them, you don't provide them electricity or gas or water or anything else . . . *A country can be attacked in a much broader way, to bring the country to the brink of dysfunction. This is the necessary outcome of events*" in Gaza.[468] He has repeatedly asserted the benefits for Israel of the creation of a humanitarian crisis in Gaza, stating that "*Israel has no interest in the Gaza Strip being rehabilitated* and this is an important point that needs to be made clear to the Americans",[469] and that "[i]f we ever want to see the hostages alive, the only way is to create a *severe humanitarian crisis in Gaza*".[470] He has indicated that water should be targeted, noting that water in Gaza "comes from wells with salt water unfit for consumption. They have water treatment plants, Israel should hit those plants. When the entire world says we have gone insane and this is a humanitarian disaster — we will say, it's not an end, it's a means."[471] In a Times radio interview on 12 October 2023, he reiterated the army should:

> "[C]reate such a huge pressure on Gaza, that Gaza will become an area where people cannot live. People cannot live, until Hamas is destroyed, which means that Israel not only stops to supply energy, diesel, water, food ... as we did in the last twenty years ... but we should prevent any possible assistance by others, and to create in Gaza such a terrible, unbearable situation, that can last weeks and months".[472]

Giora Eiland has repeatedly been given a media platform to call for Gaza to be made uninhabitable, declaring "*the State of Israel has no choice but to make Gaza a place that is temporarily, or permanently, impossible to live in.*"[473] In an interview on 6 November 2023, he suggested that, "if there is an intention for a military action at Shifa [Hospital], which I think is inescapable, I hope that the head of the CIA got an explanation of why this is necessary, and why *the US must ultimately back even an operation like this, even if there are thousands of bodies of civilians in the streets afterward.*"[474] Further he proposed that "Israel needs to create a humanitarian crisis in Gaza, compelling tens of thousands or even hundreds of thousands to seek refuge in Egypt or the Gulf . . . *Gaza will become a place where no human being can exist.*"[475] Echoing the words of President Herzog, he has repeatedly underscored that there should be no distinction between Hamas combatants and Palestinian civilians, saying:

> "Who are the 'poor' women of Gaza? *They are all the mothers, sisters or wives of Hamas murderers.* On the one hand, they are part of the infrastructure that supports the organization, and on the other hand, if they experience a humanitarian disaster, then it can be assumed that some of the Hamas fighters and the more junior commanders will begin to understand that the war is futile . . . The international community warns us of a humanitarian disaster in Gaza and of severe epidemics. We must not shy away from this, as difficult as that may be. After all, *severe epidemics in the south of the Gaza Strip will bring victory closer* . . . It is *precisely its civil collapse that will bring the end of the war closer.* When senior Israeli figures say in the media 'It's either us or them' we should clarify the question of who is 'them'. 'They' are not only Hamas fighters with weapons, but also *all the 'civilian' officials, including hospital administrators and school administrators, and also the entire Gaza population* who enthusiastically supported Hamas and cheered on its atrocities on October 7th."[476]

Israeli Army reservist "motivational speech": On 11 October 2023 95-year old Israeli

army reservist Ezra Yachin   veteran of the Deir Yassin massacre during the 1948 Nakba

called up for reserve duty to "boost morale"

broadcast on social media

dressed in Israeli army fatigues

"Be triumphant and finish them off and don't leave anyone behind *Erase the memory of*

them   Erase them their families mothers   *children*   *These animals can no longer live*

Every Jew with a weapon should go out and kill   If you have an Arab neighbour

don't wait go to his home and shoot him   We want to invade not like before we want

to enter and *destroy*   *destroy*   *destroy*

complete destruction   destroy

erase

them "

"On *the third day when they were in pain Simeon*

and Levi two of Jacob's sons brothers of Dinah took each his sword came upon the city

unmolested and slew all the males"

Commander in the 2908th Battalion of the Israeli army: In a video posted online on

21 December 2023 Yair Ben David said that the Israeli army had "entered Beit Hanoun and

did there as Shimon and Levi did in Nablus "

above statements by Israeli decision-makers and military officials indicate

clear intent to destroy Palestinians in Gaza as a group   as such   also constitute clear

direct and public incitement to genocide

also   clear   from the emerging evidence from Israeli army

soldiers serving in Gaza

Israeli Army Colonel, Deputy Head of COGAT: speaking in a video filmed in Beit

Lahia

broadcast on Israeli television on 4 November 2023 Colonel Yogev Bar-

Sheshet stated   " w hoever returns here   will find scorched earth No

houses no agriculture no nothing They have no future "

another Army Colonel recorded in

the same video Colonel Erez Eshel (Reserve)   "Vengeance is a great

value   There is vengeance over what they did to us   This place will be a fallow land   They

will not be able to live here"

Israeli soldiers in uniform   filmed on 5 December 2023

dancing chanting   singing "May their village burn May Gaza be erased"   two days

later   dancing singing   chanting

"we know our motto *there are no uninvolved civilians*   *wipe off the seed of Amalek*" non-cabinet members of the Israeli Knesset

"there are no uninvolved"   " t here are no innocents in Gaza"

"the children of Gaza have brought this upon themselves"   "there should be one sentence for

everyone   death"

have also called for "mercilessly" bombing   for the use of nuclear

weapons   a "Nakba that will overshadow the Nakba of 48"

genocidal rhetoric   commonplace in Israeli civil society   genocidal messages

routinely broadcast   call for

Gaza to be "erase d "   turned into a "slaughterhouse"

"Gaza should be razed"   " t here are *no innocents*

There are 2.5 million terrorists"

one former MK

"I tell you *in Gaza without exception they are all terrorists sons of dogs   They must be*

exterminated all of them killed   We will flatten Gaza   turn them to dust   *the army will*

cleanse the area   Then we will start building new areas   for us   for our security "

Recognition of Israel's genocidal intent against Palestinians

numerous States have   recognized Israel's

genocidal intent   assessment   shared by a significant number of United

Nations experts

On 19 October 2023 **nine United Nations Special Rapporteurs** sounded   alarm

warning

risk of genocide against the Palestinian People

On 27 October 2023   **United Nations Committee on the Elimination of Racial

Discrimination** underscored

dehumanization directed at Palestinians

including by senior officials politicians members of the

Parliament   public figures

language which could *incite genocidal actions*

On 28 October 2023 **the Director of the New York Office of the High Commissioner**

of Human Rights ('OHCHR') stepped down   penning a   resignation

describing the situation in Gaza as a *"text-book case of genocide"*

On 2 November 2023 **eight Special Rapporteurs** warned that they "remain convinced

that *the Palestinian people are at grave risk of genocide* "   " t he time

for action is now"

On 16 November 2023   **15 United Nations Special Rapporteurs and 21 members of**

United Nations Working Groups cautioned that " g rave violations committed by Israel

point to *a genocide in*

the making"   "evidence of *increasing genocidal incitement*   overt

intent to *"destroy the Palestinian people under occupation"* loud calls for a 'second Nakba'

"profound   concern   about   the *failure*

of the international system to mobilise to prevent genocide"

they called on " t he international community

to "do everything it can to *immediately end*

the risk of genocide against the Palestinian people"

On 20 November 2023, the **United Nations Special Rapporteur on violence against**

women and girls issued warning that " s ince 7

October the assault on Palestinian women's dignity and rights has taken on new and terrifying

dimensions victims of war crimes   crimes against humanity   an

unfolding genocide" alarm at the *genocidal and*

dehumanizing rhetoric about the Palestinian people

calls

for a 'second Nakba' by Israeli officials " *make the Israeli*

Government's intention to destroy the Palestinian people in whole or in part   absolutely and

consistently clear"

vetoed by the United States of America

THE RELIEF SOUGHT

prevent genocide

                                                of

Palestinians

Palestinians

            life

        persons

Palestinians in Gaza   displaced from Gaza

reparation

safe and dignified return

respect

protection

Nowhere is safe in Gaza

Palestinians in Gaza are being killed

                      killed

              children   killed

                  wounded daily

Besieged and bombed

forcibly displaced

                imminent mass starvation

Israel denies wrongdoing

Israel has continued   escalated   threatened

It is also destroying evidence of its wrongdoing

shared values

erga omnes partes

erga omnes partes

erga omnes partes

rights   *erga omnes* obligations

obligations not to commit genocide to prevent genocide

to punish genocide

to liberate mankind from such an odious scourge

there is urgency

urgency

urgency

genocide

population

vulnerable

extremely

vulnerable

a ttacks are ongoing

attacks

systematic

stripping of human rights   dehumanizing narratives and rhetoric   methodical planning   mass

killing   mass displacement   mass fear   overwhelming levels of brutality

physical destruction of the home of the targeted population in every sense and on every level

South Africa

respectfully requests the Court as a matter of

extreme urgency   to indicate the following

provisional measures

The State of Israel shall immediately suspend its military operations in and against Gaza

The Republic of South Africa and the State of Israel shall each

take all reasonable measures within their power to prevent

genocide

The State of Israel shall

in relation to the Palestinian people

desist from

killing

causing serious bodily or mental harm

deliberately inflicting   conditions of life calculated to bring about its

physical destruction   and

imposing measures intended to prevent births within the group

The State of Israel shall   in relation to Palestinians desist

from

          expulsion   forced displacement

          deprivation of

                    food and water

                                        fuel shelter

          clothes hygiene   sanitation

              medical supplies and assistance

          destruction of Palestinian life in Gaza

Israel shall

not

commit genocide

Israel shall

ensure the

preservation of evidence

NOTES

[1] Convention on the Prevention and Punishment of the Crime of Genocide (adopted 9 December 1948, entered into force 12 January 1951), 78 UNTS 277. [2] Raphaël Lemkin, *Axis Rule in Occupied Europe: Laws of Occupation, Analysis of Government Proposals for Redress* (1944), Chapter IX. [3] Geneva Convention Relative to the Protection of Civilian Persons in Time of War, 12 August 1949, 75 UNTS 287. [4] Speech by Mahmoud Abbas on Palestine TV, 18 November 2023, https://www.youtube.com/watch?v=2uRGx02vULg; translated by WAFA: "President Abbas urges Biden to stop Israel's ongoing genocide of Palestinians", *WAFA* (18 November 2023), https://english.wafa.ps/Pages/Details/139394. [5] United Nations Office of the High Commissioner for Human Rights ('UN OHCHR'), *Gaza: UN experts decry bombing of hospitals and schools as crimes against humanity, call for prevention of genocide* (19 October 2023) https://www.ohchr.org/en/press-releases/2023/10/gaza-un-experts-decry-bombing-hospitals-and-schools-crimes-against-humanity. [6] UN OHCHR, *Gaza: UN experts call on international community to prevent genocide against the Palestinian people* (16 November 2023), https://www.ohchr.org/en/press-releases/2023/11/gaza-un-experts-call-international-community-preventgenocide-against. [7] UN OHCHR *Gaza Strip: States are obliged to prevent crimes against humanity and genocide, UN Com mittee stresses* (21 December 2023) https://www.ohchr.org/en/press-releases/2023/12/gaza-strip-states-are-obliged-prevent-crimes-againsthumanity-and-genocide. Under CERD's Early Warning and Urgent Action ('EWUA') procedure, CERD has extensive expertise in compiling indicators relevant to the prevention of genocide; in 2015 it issued a Declaration on the Prevention of Genocide which recalled this work in its preamble: see CERD, *Declaration on the Prevention of Genocide* (CRD/C/66/1) (17 October 2005), https://www.ohchr.org/sites/default/files/Documents/ HRBodies/CERD/declaration_genocide.doc (emphasis added). [8] *Application of the Convention on the Prevention and Punishment of the Crime of Genocide (The Gambia v. Myanmar), Provisional Measures, Order of 23 January 2020, I.C.J. Reports 2020*, p. 14, para. 30 (hereafter '*The Gambia v. Myanmar, Provisional Measures, Order of 23 January 2020*'). [9] "Algeria, Türkiye discuss need for accountability over Gaza 'genocide'", *Middle East Monitor* (21 November 2023), https://www.middleeastmonitor.com/20231121 -algeria-president-tebboune-turkiye-president-erdogan-discuss-need-foraccountability-over-gaza-genocide/. The People's Democratic Republic of Algeria acceded to the Genocide Convention on 31 October 1963. [10] Luis Alberto Arce Catacora (Lucho Arce), Presidente Constitucional del Estado Plurinacional de Bolivia, @LuchoXBolivia, Tweet (2:43 am, November 16, 2023), https://twitter.com/LuchoXBolivia/status/ 1724981446001967283. The Plurinational State of Bolivia signed the Genocide Convention on 11 December 1948 and ratified it on 14 June 2005. [11] "President Lula says war in the Middle East is genocide", *AgenciaBrazil* (25 October 2023), https:// agenciabrasil.ebc. com.br/en/politica/noticia/2023-10/president-lula-says-war-middle-east-genocide. The Federative Republic of Brazil signed the Genocide Convention on 11 December 1948 and ratified it on 15 April 1952. [12] Gustavo Petro, Presidente de la República de Colombia, @petrogustavo, Tweet (4:00 am, November 1, 2023) https://twitter.com/petrogustavo/status/1719565081371935150. The Republic of Colombia signed the Genocide Convention on 12 August 1949 and ratified it 27 October 1959. [13] Ed Newman, "Diaz-Canel says Cuba will not accept ignoring genocide against Palestinians", *Radio Havana Cuba* (29 October 2023), https://www.radiohc.cu/en/noticias/ nacionales/337800-diaz-canel-says-cuba-will-not-accept-ignoringgenocide-against-palestinians. The Republic of Cuba signed the Genocide Convention on 28 December 1949 and ratified it on 4 March 1953. [14] "Iranian president condemns Gaza 'genocide' in meeting with Putin", *NBC News* (7 December 2023), https://www.nbcnews.com/video/iranian-president-condemns-gaza-genocide-in-meeting-with-putin-199670853701. The Islamic Republic of Iran signed the Genocide Convention on 8 December 1949 and ratified it on 14 August 1956. [15] Recep Tayyip Erdoğan, President of Türkiye and AK Party Chairman, @RTErdogan, Tweet, (4:30 pm, 18 October 2023), https://twitter.com/RTErdogan/status/1714665167978369531. The Republic of Türkiye acceded to the Genocide Convention on 31 July 1950. [16] Nicolás Maduro, Presidente de la República Bolivariana de Venezuela, @NicolasMaduro, Tweet (7:40 pm, November 4, 2023) https://twitter.com/NicolasMaduro/status/1720888719568191585. The Bolivarian Republic of Venezuela acceded to the Genocide Convention on 12 July 1960. [17] "President Abbas urges Biden to stop Israel's ongoing genocide of Palestinians", *WAFA* (18 November 2023), https://english.wafa.ps/Pages/Details/139394. The State of Palestine acceded to the Genocide Convention on 2 April 2014. [18] UN, Meetings Coverage and Press Releases, Seventy-Eighth Session, 39th and 40th Meetings, GA/12566, *Staggering Loss of Life in Gaza, Follow-on to Temporary Truce Dominate General Assembly Debate on Decades-Long Question of Palestine*, GA/12566 (28 November 2023), https://press.un.org/en/2023/ga12566.doc.htm. The People's Republic of Bangladesh acceded to the Genocide Convention on 5 October 1998. [19] UN News, *UN General Assembly adopts Gaza resolution calling for immediate and sustained 'humanitarian truce'* (26 October 2023), https://news.un.org/en/story/2023/10/1142847. The Arab Republic of Egypt signed the Genocide Convention on 12 December 1948 and ratified the Convention on 8 February 1952. [20] "Live updates | Israel rebuffs US push for humanitarian pause, says hostages must be released first", *Associated Press* (3 November 2023), https://web.archive.org/web/20231117082155/https://thehill.com/homenews/ap/ap-international/ap-live-updates-israeli-troops-tighten-encirclement-of-gaza-city-as-top-us-diplomat-arrivesin-israel/. The Republic of Honduras signed the Genocide Convention on 22 April 1949 and ratified the Convention on 5 March 1952. [21] "Israel subjects Palestinians 'to genocide,' says Sudani", *Rudaw* (6 November 2023), https://www.rudaw.net/english/middleeast/06112023. The Republic of Iraq acceded to the Genocide Convention on 20 January 1959. [22] "Jordan's foreign minister says Israel aiming 'to empty Gaza of its people'", *AlJazeera* (10 December 2023), https://www.aljazeera.com/news/2023/12/10/jordan-foreign-minister-says-israel-aiming-to-empty-gaza-of-its-people. The Hashemite Kingdom of Jordan acceded to the Genocide Convention on 3 April 1950. [23] UN, Meetings Coverage and Press Releases, 9451st Meeting, SC/15462, *Amid Increasingly Dire Humanitarian Situation in Gaza, Secretary-General Tells Security Council Hamas Attacks Cannot Justify Collective Punishment of Palestinian People* (24 October 2023), https://press. un.org/en/2023/sc15462.doc.htm. The State of Libya acceded to the Genocide Convention on 16 May 1989.

54 General Assembly resolution ES-10/22, Protection of civilians and upholding legal and humanitarian obligations, A/RES/ES-10/22 (12 December 2023), https://www.un.org/unispal/wp-content/uploads/2023/12/N2339709.

55 The Secretary-General, Letter by the Secretary-General to the President of Security Council invoking Article, United Nations Charter (6 December 2023), https://www.un.org/sites/un2.un.org/files/sg_letter_of_6_decem.

56 UN OCHA, Hostilities in the Gaza Strip and Israel | Flash Update #78 (27 December 2023), https://www.ochaopt.org/content/hostilities-gaza-strip-and-israel-flash-update-78 ; UN OCHA, Hostilities in the Gaza Strip and Israel – reported impact | Day 82 (27 December 2023), https://www.ochaopt.org/content/hostilities-gaza-strip-and-israel-reported-impact-day-82. Statistics cited in this Application are up to date to 27 December 2023.

57 UN OCHA, Hostilities in the Gaza Strip and Israel | Flash Update #78 (27 December 2023), https://www.ochaopt.org/content/hostilities-gaza-strip-and-israel-flash-update-78.

58 Red Crescent Society, Palestine Red Crescent Society Response Report As of Sunday, December 24th 2023, 24:00 AM (24 December 2023), https://www.palestinercs.org/public/files/image/2023.

59 UN OCHA, Hostilities in the Gaza Strip and Israel | Flash Update #77 (26 December 2023), https://www.ochaopt.org/content/hostilities-gaza-strip-and-israel-flash-update-77.

60 UN OCHA, Hostilities in the Gaza Strip and Israel | Flash Update #60 (5 December 2023), https://www.ochaopt.org/content/hostilities-gaza-strip-and-israel-flash-update-60.

61 UN OCHA, Hostilities in the Gaza Strip and Israel | Flash Update #78 (27 December 2023), https://www.ochaopt.org/content/hostilities-gaza-strip-and-israel-flash-update-78.

62 UN News, Gaza: UN's Türk calls for political path out of 'horror' (16 November 2023), https://news.un.org/en/story/2023/11/143657.

63 UN OCHA, Hostilities in the Gaza Strip and Israel | Flash Update #32; UN News, Interview (November 2023), https://news.un.org/en/interview/2023/11/1143327.

64 UN News, Gaza doctors 'terrified' of deadly disease outbreak as aid teams race to deliver (28 November 2023), https://news.un.org/en/story/2023/11/1144032.

65 World Health Organization ('WHO'), WHO Director-General's opening remarks at the Special Session of the Executive Board on the health situation in the occupied Palestinian territory (10 December 2023), https://www.who.int/director-general/speeches/detail/who-director-general-s-opening-remarks-at-the-special-session-of-the-executive-board-on-the-health-situation-in-the-occupied-palestinian-territory--10-december-2023; UN OCHA, Hostilities in the Gaza Strip and Israel | Flash Update #67 (12 December 2023), https://www.ochaopt.org/content/hostilities-gaza-strip-and-israel-flash-update-67.

66 UN OCHA, Hostilities in the Gaza Strip and Israel | Flash Update #77 (26 December 2023), https://www.ochaopt.org/content/hostilities-gaza-strip-and-israel-flash-update-77; UN OCHA, Remarks by the media Secretary-General (22 December 2023), https://www.ochaopt.org/content/remarks-media-secretary-general.

67 Interview with James Elder, UNICEF spokesperson by Channel 4, "This is a war on children" says James Elder, who recently returned from Gaza", Channel 4 (14 December 2023), https://www.channel4.com/news/this-is-a-war-on-children-says-unicef-spokesperson-james-elder-who-recently-returned-from-gaza; "Disease could kill more in Gaza than bombs, WHO says amid Israeli siege", AlJazeera (28 November 2023), https://www.aljazeera.com/news/2023/11/28/disease-could-kill-more-in-gaza-than-bombs-who-says.

68 General Assembly resolution ES-10/22, Protection of civilians and upholding legal and humanitarian obligations, A/RES/ES-10/22 (12 December 2023), https://www.un.org/unispal/wp-content/uploads/2023/12/N.

69 General Assembly resolution ES-10/21, Protection of civilians and upholding legal and humanitarian obligations (30 October 2023), https://www.un.org/unispal/document/protection-of-civilians-and-upholding-legal-resolution-a-res-es-10-21/.

75 UN OCHA, Hostilities in the Gaza Strip and Israel – reported impact | Day 73 (19 December 2023), https://www.ochaopt.org/content/hostilities-gaza-strip-and-israel-reported-impact-day-73.

76 UN OCHA, Israel must rescind evacuation order for northern Gaza and comply with international humanitarian law (13 October 2023), https://www.ochaopt.org/content/israel-must-rescind-evacuation-order; OHCHR, Israel must rescind evacuation order (13 October 2023), https://www.ohchr.org/en/press-releases/2023/10/israel-must-rescind-evacu.

78 ibid.

70 UNRWA, Letter from UNRWA Commissioner-General Philippe Lazzarini to the UN General Assembly, Commissioner-General Philippe Lazzarini dated 7 December 2023 (7 December 2023), https://www.unrwa.org/resources/reports/letter-commissioner-general-philippe-lazzarini-un-general-assembly (emphasis added).

71 General Assembly resolution 67/19, Status of Palestine in the United Nations, A/RES/67/19, https://digitallibrary.un.org/record/739031/files/A_RES_67_19-EN.pdf. 82 States had recognised the State of Palestine.

127 International Criminal Court, Statement of ICC Prosecutor Karim A. A. Khan KC from Cairo on the situation in the State of Palestine and Israel (30 October 2023), https://www.icc-cpi.int/news/statement-icc-prosecutor-karim-khan-kc-cairo-situation-state-palestine-and-israel ; International Criminal Court, @IntlCrimCourt (4:08 p.m, October 29, 2023), https://twitter.com/intlcrimcourt/status/1718661091155161172?s=46&t=bZu5nJejRUuojpOH1KVB5Q.
128 International Criminal Court, Statement of ICC Prosecutor Karim A. A. Khan KC from Cairo on the situation in the State of Palestine and Israel (30 October 2023), https://www.icc-cpi.int/news/statement-icc-prosecutor-karim-khan-kc-cairo-situation-state-palestine-and-israel
129 Ibid.
130 South Africa, Embassy in the Netherlands, Letter from the South African Embassy in the
Palestine-Final-17-November-2023.pdf, the fact that the Prosecutor has not yet completed any investigation
prosecution in relation to the Situation in the State of Palestine since 31 January, 2021, nor opened an investigation
in response to the referral of genocide by South Africa and others, is no bar to the ICJ determining the present
Notably, the ICC's investigation is to determine individual criminal responsibility for the crime of genocide, contrast
Rome Statute of the International Criminal Court, whereas the ICJ's jurisdiction is to determine disputes
responsibility for genocide under the Genocide Convention.
131 UN Palestine, Israeli Occupation of Palestinian Territory in facts and figures

ing family", *The Guardian* (22 December 2023), https://www.theguardian.com/world/2023/dec/22/the-plight-of-gazas-wensfs-wounded-chil...

Yamina Boukari, James Smith and Amy Neilson, "The health in Palestine: a call to prevent genocide", *The Lancet* (18 December 2023), https://www.thelancet.com/journals/lancet/article/PIIS0140-6736(23)02751-4/fulltext

UN Security Council, Resolution 2712, The situation in the Middle East, including the Palestinian Question, S/RES/2712 (15 ...), https://undocs.org/S/RES/2712(2023)

UN OCHA, *Hostilities in the Gaza Strip and Israel | Flash Update #78* (27 December 2023), https://www.ochaopt.org/content/hostilities-gaza-strip-and-israel-flash-update-78

Shannon, Khudejha Ashgar, Yamina Boukari, James Smith and Amy Neilson, "The health in Palestine: a call to prevent genocide", *The Lancet* (18 December 2023), https://www.thelancet.com/journals/lancet/article/PIIS0140-6736(23)02751-4/fulltext

"An aid worker describes the 'unbearable' suffering of wounded children in Gaza", *NPR* (26 December 2023), https://www.npr.org/2023/12/26/1221743518/an-aid-worker-describes-the-unbearable-suffering-of-wounded-...

OHCHR, "UN human rights office alarmed at Israeli strikes on or in the vicinities of schools and hospitals in the north of Gaza", https://www.ohchr.org/en/press-releases/... un-human-rights-office-ohchr-alarmed-israeli-...

"Gaza healthcare workers 'taken' by Israeli forces, says doctor, amid 'horrendous conditions' at hospitals", *CNN* (13 December 2023), https://edition.cnn.com/2023/12/13/middleeast/gaza-kamal-adwan-hospital-doctors-idf-intl/index.html

UN OCHA, *Hostilities in the Gaza Strip and Israel | Flash Update #77* (26 December 2023), https://www.ochaopt.org/content/hostilities-gaza-strip-and-israel-flash-update-77; Quds News Network, @QudsNen, Tweet (6:02 pm, December 25, 2023), https://twitter.com/QudsNen/status/1739315746163859606

UN OCHA, *Hostilities in the Gaza Strip and Israel | Flash Update #69* (14 December 2023), https://www.ochaopt.org/content/hostilities-gaza-strip-and-israel-flash-update-69; UN OCHA, *Hostilities in the Gaza Strip and Israel | Flash Update #77* (26 December 2023), https://www.ochaopt.org/content/hostilities-gaza-strip-and-israel-flash-update-77.

Ibid.

See e.g. Yaniv Kubovich, "Graphic Videos and Incitement: How the IDF Is Misleading Israelis on Telegram", *Haaretz* (12 December 2023), https://www.haaretz.com/israel-news/security-aviation/2023-12-12/ty-article/premium/graphic-videos-and-incitement-how-the-idf-is-misleading-israelis-on-telegram/0000018c-5ab5-df2f-adac-febd01c30000

UN OCHA, *Hostilities in the Gaza Strip and Israel - reported impact | Day #82* (27 December 2023), https://www.ochaopt.org/content/hostilities-gaza-strip-and-israel-reported-impact-day-82.

Israeli Defence Forces, @IDF, Tweet (6:50am, October 13, 2023), https://twitter.com/IDF/status/1712707301369434398; OHCHR, *Israel must rescind evacuation order for northern Gaza and comply with international law, UN expert* (13 October 2023), https://www.ohchr.org/en/press-releases/2023/10/israel-must-rescind-evacuation-order-northern-gaza-and-comply-international

ICRC, *Israel and the occupied territories: Evacuation order of Gaza triggers catastrophic humanitarian consequences* (October 2023), https://www.icrc.org/en/document/israel-and-occupied-territories-evacuation-order-of-gaza-triggers-catastrophic-humanitarian-consequences

WHO, *Evacuation orders by Israel to hospitals in northern Gaza area deadly...* (... 2023), https://www.who.int/news/...

UN OCHA, *Hostilities in the Gaza Strip and Israel | Flash Update #57* (2 December 2023), https://www.ochaopt.org/content/hostilities-gaza-strip-and-israel-flash-update-57

Israeli Defence Forces, @IDF, Tweet (2:16 pm, October 28, 2023), https://twitter.com/IDF/status/1718240244129059161

UN OCHA, *Hostilities in the Gaza Strip and Israel | Flash Update #40* (15 November 2023), https://www.ochaopt.org/content/hostilities-gaza-strip-and-israel-flash-update-40; UN OCHA, *Today's top news: Occupied ...*, https://www.unocha.org/news/todays-top-news-...

UN OCHA, *Hostilities in the Gaza Strip and Israel | Flash Update #56* (1 December 2023), https://www.ochaopt.org/content/hostilities-gaza-strip-and-israel-flash-update-56.

UN OCHA, *Hostilities in the Gaza Strip and Israel | Flash Update #63* (8 December 2023), https://www.ochaopt.org/content/hostilities-gaza-strip-and-israel-flash-update-63

UNRWA, *Gaza: UNRWA school sheltering displaced families is hit* (17 October 2023), https://www.unrwa.org/newsroom/official-statements/gaza-unrwa-school-sheltering-displaced-families-hit

UN Secretary-General, *Statement attributable to the Spokesperson for the Secretary-General – on the Middle East* (4 December 2023), https://www.un.org/sg/en/content/sg/statement/2023-12-04/statement-attributable-the-spokesperson-for-the-secretary-general-%E2%80%93-the-middle-east

Thomas White, @TomWhiteGaza, Tweet (9:22 AM, December 23, 2023), https://twitter.com/TomWhiteGaza/status/1738475273522203552?ref_src=twsrc%5Etfw

See, e.g. Israeli strikes on Deir Al Balah on 4 December, preceding civilians being told to flee to these areas, UN OCHA, *Hostilities in the Gaza Strip and Israel | Flash Update #60* (5 December 2023), https://www.ochaopt.org/content/hostilities-gaza-strip-and-israel-flash-update-60; and on the 12th of December 2023 the City of Rafah, after evacuation orders to Rafah, following civilians being told to flee to these areas, Ben van der Merwe, Michelle Inez Simon Olive Enokido-Lineham, and Data & Forensics Unit, "Israel said Gazans could flee to this neighbourhood - then it was hit", *Sky News* (22 December 2023), https://news.sky.com/story/israel-said-gazans-could-flee-to-this-neighbourhood-then-it-was-hit-13014936

UN OHCHR, *Comment by...* Human Rights...

Acknowledgments

This book has been a departure from my usual writing, and it would not have been possible without the guidance and support of many friends who read early drafts and offered sage counsel. I am grateful to Peter Cole, Richard Deming, Tyehimba Jess, and Nathan Nikolic. Ammiel Alcalay deserves special mention as a generous reader and as a guiding light in a dark world—a true organic intellectual who has focused his talents as scholar, critic, poet, translator, and organizer on the plight of Palestinians in Gaza.

Three erasures in these pages first appeared in *ANMLY #38*. I am grateful to Anomalous Press, and to editor Sarah Clark, for their early support of the project and for granting reprint permission. Yale University offered publication support through the Whitney Humanities Center's Hilles Fund and through the Dean's Office of the Faculty of Arts and Sciences. For this I thank Diane Brown, Marta Figlerowicz, and Thomas Connolly of the Hilles Publication Fund Committee, as well as Marc Robinson, Dean of Humanities. For helping me think about erasure and visual poetry in new ways, I am grateful to the K-12 teachers in my seminar "Poetry as Sound and Object," taught through the Yale-New Haven Teachers Institute and the Yale National Initiative.

Everyone at Brick Books has been simply wonderful, and I thank all who brought this project to fruition: River Halen, Sonnet L'Abbé, Manahil Bandukwala, and Natalie Olsen. Alayna Munce has nurtured this book with great care at every step of the publishing process. My every fiber thanks Jordan Abel, whose work is an inspiration and who found the time amongst his many commitments to serve as editor. His keen-sighted advice was always on the mark.

As ever, I am grateful above all to my wife, Sally Fattah. Sharing the wandering course with her is the joy of my life.

In lieu of author royalties, a donation will be made to the United Nations Relief and Works Agency for Palestine Refugees in the Near East (UNRWA).

Feisal G. Mohamed is a professor of English at Yale University with degrees in biology, English, and law. A past president of the Milton Society of America, his most recent books are *Sovereignty* (2020) and *Resistance* (forthcoming). In addition to academic venues, his writing has appeared in *The New York Times*, *Dissent Magazine*, *the Chronicle Review*, *The Yale Review*, *The American Scholar*, *Huffington Post*, and *Boston Review*. He grew up in Edmonton, Alberta and now lives in Connecticut with his family.